Animals

Lion  Лев

Dog  пес

Cat  кіт

Monkey  мавпа

Giraffe  жираф

Wolf  вовк

Animals

Bear  **ведмідь**

fish  **риба**

crocodile  **крокодил**

chicken  **курка**

cow  **корова**

bunny  **зайчик**

English Learning

For Ukrainian Kids

Let's learn English!!!

Bilingual Book

Learn – Color – Write

At home

window   вікно

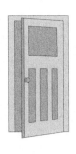

Door   двері

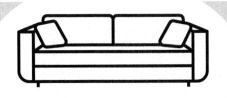

Furniture   меблі

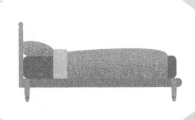

Bed   ліжко курка

Chair   стілець

Kitchen   кухня зайчик

At home

Toilet		**туалет**
Bookshelf		**книжкова полиця**
TV		**телевізор**
Clock		**Годинник**
Table		**стіл**
Kitchen	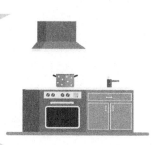	*кухня* **зайчик**

At School

Pen  ~~туалет~~ *ручка*

Ruler  лінійка

Backpack  рюкзак

Students  студентів

School  школа

Classroom  класній кімнаті

At School

Book  книга

Notebook  блокнот

Eraser
Rubber  гумка

Calculator  калькулятор

Scissors  ножиці

Pencil case  пенал

outside

Park  парк

Jungle  джунглі

Bus  автобус

Car  автомобіль

Stadium  стадіон

House  будинок

outside

Road		**дорога**
Sky		**небо**
Airplane		**літак**
People		**Люди**
Restaurant		**ресторан**
Coffee shop		**кав'ярня**

outside

buildings — будівель

Traffic sign — Дорожній знак

crosswalk — пішохідний перехід

pharmacy — АПТЕКА

Bicycle — Велосипед

garbage — сміття

Food and drinks

Fruits  Фрукти

vegetables  овочі

Barbecue  Барбекю

Beef  Яловичина

Bread  Хліб

Burger  Бургери

Food and drinks

Cheese		сир
Chicken		курка
Coffee		кава
Egg		яйце
Apple		яблуко
Watermelon		Кавун

Food and drinks

Orange		Помаранчевий
Pear		груша
Cherry		Вишня
Strawberry		Полуниця
Nectarine		Нектарин
Grape		Виноградний

Food and drinks

Mango		манго
Plum		Сливовий
Banana		банан
Kiwi		ківі
Pineapple		ананас
Lemon		Лимонний

Food and drinks

Apricot  Абрикосови

Grapefruit  грейпфру т

Melon  Диня

Coconut  кокос

Avocado  авокадо

Peach  Персиковий

Food and drinks

Corn 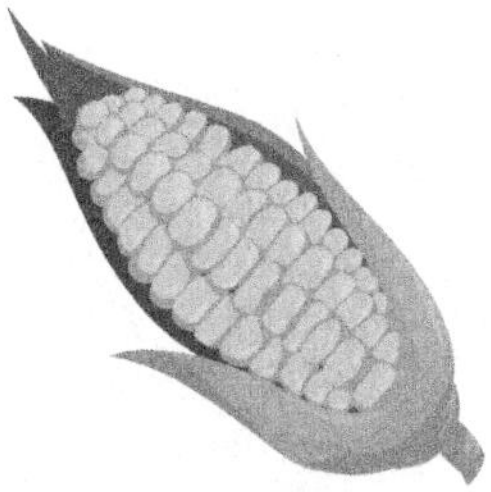   Кукурудза

Mushroom    Гриб

Broccoli    Брокколі

Cucumber    огірок

Tomato    Томатний

Carrot 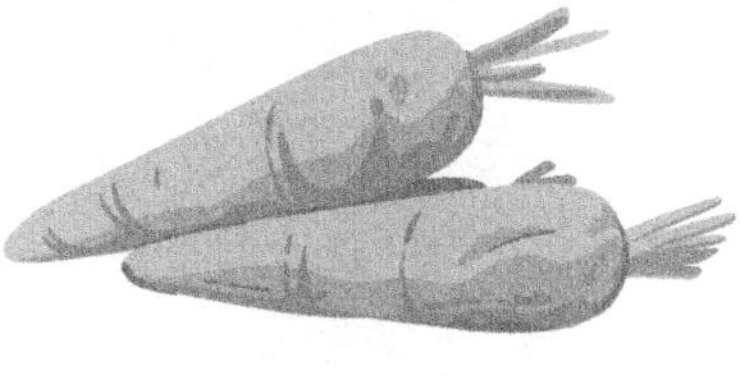   Морква

Food and drinks

Pumpkin  Гарбуз

Cabbage  Капуста

Potato  Картопля

Eggplant 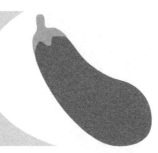 Баклажани

Sweet
potato  Солодка
картопля

Turnip  ріпа

Food and drinks

Onion		**Цибуля**
Lettuce		**салат**
Radish		**Редька**
Celery		**Селера**
Pepper		**перець**
Bean		**Бобові**

Food and drinks

Lemonade   Лимонад

chocolate   салат

Juice   Сік

Water   Вода

Tea   Чай

Milk   Молоко

Professions and jobs

Accountant		**бухгалтер**
Actor		**актор**
Architect		**архітектор**
Artist		**художник**
Banker		**банкір**
Barber		**цирульник**

Professions and jobs

Builder  будівельни

Businessman  бізнесмен

Butcher  м'ясник

Carpenter  столяр

Chef  шеф-кухар

Coach  тренер

Professions and jobs

Dentist  **стоматолог**

Doctor  **лікар**

Economist  **економіст**

Editor  **редактор**

Electrician  **електрик**

Engineer  **інженер**

Professions and jobs

Farmer		фермер
Fisherman		рибалка
Flight attendant		стюардеса
Jeweler		ювелір
Lawyer		юрист
Mechanic		механік

Professions and jobs

Musician		**музикант**
Nurse		**медсестра**
Optician		**оптик**
Painter		**живописець**
Pharmacist		**фармацевт**
Photographer		**фотограф**

Professions and jobs

Pilot		пілот
Plumber		сантехнік
Police officer		офіцер поліції
Politician		політик
Professor		професор
Programmer		програміст

Professions and jobs

Secretary  секретар

Singer  співачка

Teacher  вчитель

Veterinarian  ветеринар

Waiter  офіціант

Writer  письменник

Family

Father		**батько**
Mother		**мати**
Son		**син**
Daughter		**дівчина**
Brothers		**братів**
Sisters		**сестри**

Family

Man  чоловіків

Women  жінки

Boys  Хлопчики

Girls  дочка

Grandfather  дідусь

Grandmother  бабуся

Numbers

English		Ukrainian
One	1	один
Two	2	Два
Three	3	Три
Four	4	Чотири
Five	5	п'ять
Six	6	шість
Seven	7	Сім
Eight	8	вісім
Nine	9	дев'ять
Ten	10	десять

Day of the week

English	Ukrainian
Sunday	неділя
Monday	понеділок
Tuesday	вівторок
Wednesday	середа
Thursday	четвер
Friday	п'ятниця
Saturday	субота

Months of the year

January		січня
February		лютий
march		марш
April		квітень
May		може
June		червень

Months of the year

uly	липень
August	серпень
September	Вересень
October	жовтень
November	Листопад
December	Грудень

Season

Spring весна

Summer літо

Autumn осінь

Winter зима

Clothes

lipFlops	в'єтнамки
Sock	шкарпетки
Dress	Сукня
Men Shoes	чоловіче взуття
Bathrobe	халат
JackeT	Жакет

Clothes

Vest  жилетка

Sweater  светр

Pantalon  Штани

Shirt  сорочка

Jean  джинси

Beanie  шапка

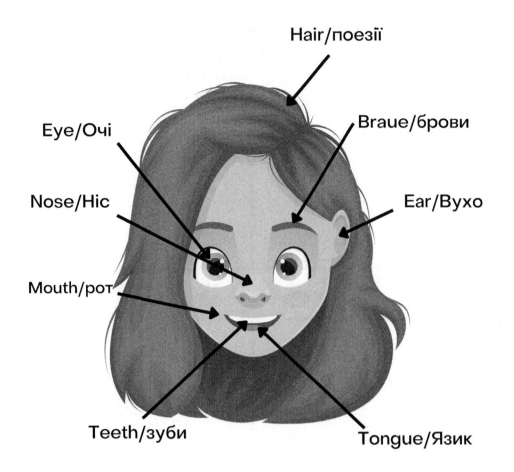

Hair/поезії

Braue/брови

Ear/Вухо

Eye/Очі

Nose/Hic

Mouth/рот

Teeth/зуби

Tongue/Язик

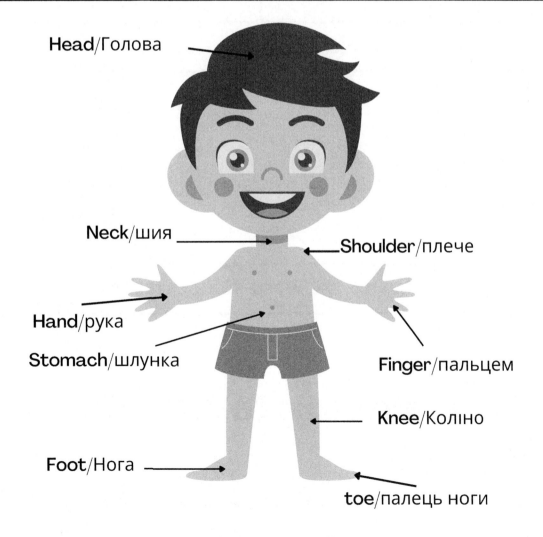

Head/Голова

Neck/шия

Shoulder/плече

Hand/рука

Stomach/шлунка

Finger/пальцем

Knee/Коліно

Foot/Нога

toe/палець ноги

Color the word

I   Я

Find and circle the word

I speak english

I went to the market

I am hungry

I   above

last

no

I   I   if

Understand the word

I am eating

Write the word in a sentence

I'm traveling to the village

Color the word

Act

 Дійте

Find and circle the word

Act normally until you find the opportunity

Act like you

Act of service

Act   with   Hug   can   Act   cook   Act

Understand the word

Act like a nurse

Write the word in a sentence

 **right**

Color the word

Run	Біжи

Find and circle the word

Run away	run
Run out of petrol	with
Run in the garden	run
	can
	Act
	run
	Act

Understand the word

Run out of money

I run

Write the word in a sentence

Color the word

| Drink | Випити |

Find and circle the word

He drinks water

he drinks milk

She drinks juice

Act with drinks drinks Act drinks cook

Understand the word

I drink

Write the word in a sentence

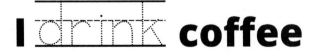 **coffee**

Color the word

Find and circle the word

I give you

I give a promise

I give you the money

Act   with

give

give

drinks   give

cook

Understand the word

I give you a book

Write the word in a sentence

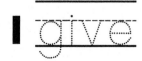

Color the word

Study

Вивчення

Find and circle the word

Study time

I study at the University of manchester

I'm studying English

study
with
give
study
drinks
cook
studying

Understand the word

I study

Write the word in a sentence

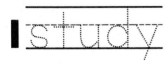 at school in Spanish

Color the word

Watch | # ДИВИТИСЯ

Find and circle the word

Watch the clock

Watch your language

You need to watch him - he's a strange

Watch   with

        Watch

    study

Watch   studying

    cook

Understand the word

I watch tv

Write the word in a sentence

 **this space**

Color the word

Approve

Затвердити

Find and circle the word

She doesn't approve of my friends

I wish my mother approved of my friends

I don't approve of that kind of language

approved

with

approve

approve

Watch

cook

studying

Understand the word

My request has been approved

Write the word in a sentence

He doesn't approve *of smoking*

Color the word

Dream

Мрія

Find and circle the word

I often dream about flying.

I dream of living on a tropical island.

It was his dream to be a football player

dream

with

dream

approve

Watch

cook

dream

Understand the word

I dream of...

Write the word in a sentence

Someone would not dream of doing something

Color the word

Sew

Шити

Find and circle the word

My grandmother taught me to sew

Do you like to sew?

She sewed her outfit by hand

sew
with
sew
approve
sewed
cook
studying

Understand the word

She sews all her children's clothes

Write the word in a sentence

I had to sew up a hole in my jeans.

Color the word

Find and circle the word

We watched a flock of birds fly over the fiel

A swarm of bees flew into the garden

We enjoy watching the birds fly over the water

fly

with

fly

flew

sewed

cook

studying

Understand the word

Birds fly in the sky

Write the word in a sentence

There isn't really enough wind to fly a kite today.

Color the word

Solve

Вирішити

Find and circle the word

To solve a problem

Wars never solve anything

Shouting won't solve anything

solve   with

solve

flew

sewed   cook   solve

Understand the word

We solved the puzzle

Write the word in a sentence

The police are still no nearer to solving the crime

Color the word

 Walk Прогулянка

Find and circle the word

I walk to work every morning

You can walk it in half an hour

I walked home

walk with
solve
flew
walk walked
cook

Understand the word

I walk ...

Write the word in a sentence

She walks **the dog for an hour every afternoon.**

Color the word

Jump

стрибати

Find and circle the word

A parachute jump

The cats jumped up onto the table

Can you jump this fence?

walk   jumped   solve

flew

jump   cook   jump

Understand the word

I jump

Write the word in a sentence

The cats jumped **up onto the table.**

Color the word

Answer

відповісти

Find and circle the word

There's no easy answer to the problem

I phoned last night but nobody answered

I think I got most of the answers right on the exam

walk   jumped
                    solve
        answered

answers   answer
        cook

Understand the word

I don't know the answer

Write the word in a sentence

I answered *the question*

Color the word

Clap	Хлопайте

Find and circle the word

People will clap at the end of a speech

She clapped her hands to call the dog in

Everyone was clapping and cheering

clapping   jumped

solve

answer

clapped   cook   clap

Understand the word

I clap my hands

Write the word in a sentence

"When I clap **my hands, you stand still," said the teacher.**

Color the word

Win

Виграти

Find and circle the word

She would do anything to win his love

Did they win last night?

Our team won the game!

win

jumped

win

answer

won

cook

clap

Understand the word

I won the cup

Write the word in a sentence

Brazil are favourites to ⎯win⎯ this year's World Cup

Color the word

Write

Пишіть

Find and circle the word

She writes children's books

Please write your name on the dotted line.

He writes well and is always a pleasure to read

writes

jumped

win

write

won

writes

cook

Understand the word

I write...

Write the word in a sentence

To write ***a poem***

Color the word

Sleep

CoH

Find and circle the word

She fell into a lovely deep sleep

I was too excited to sleep much that night

I couldn't sleep because of all the noise next door

writes   sleep
                      win
        sleep
won   sleep
      cook

Understand the word

I sleep...

Write the word in a sentence

Sleep *tight - see you in the morning.*

Color the word

Close

закрити

Find and circle the word

The museum closes at 5.30

She closed the meeting with a short speech

The factory closed over ten years ago

closes

no

win

sleep

closed

closed

cook

Understand the word

She closes the door

Write the word in a sentence

I closed **that bank account when I came to London**

Color the word

Plan	План

Find and circle the word

Holiday plans

What are your plans for this weekend?

Events of this type rarely go according to plan

break   no

plans

plans

plan   about

cook

Understand the word

I plan...

Write the word in a sentence

She helped them to plan their route

Color the word	
# Smell	# Запах

Find and circle the word

My hands smell of onions

That cake smells good

You smell lovely - what's your perfume?

smell   no   smell

plans

smells   cook   about

Understand the word

These socks smell foul!

Write the word in a sentence

This milk smells **funny**

Color the word

Dance

Танцюй

Find and circle the word

Can you dance the tango?

He was too shy to ask her to dance with him

Who was she dancing with at the party?

break   no

dance

dance

plan   about

dancing

Understand the word

I am dancing

Write the word in a sentence

Do you take dance lessons?

Color the word

Buy

Купуйте

Find and circle the word

I need to buy some new shoes

She was saving to buy a car.

We always buy paper from the same supplier

buy   no

buy

dance

plan   about

buy

Understand the word

She is buying a new car

Write the word in a sentence

This jacket is a really good

Color the word

Cut   розрізати

Find and circle the word

Cut the meat up into small pieces

This knife doesn't cut very well.

Where did you have your hair cut?

Cut   Cut
                    buy
        dance

plan   about
        Cut

Understand the word

The barber cut my hair

Write the word in a sentence

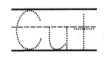 **the apple in half**

Color the word

See

Побачити

Find and circle the word

Turn the light on so I can see

I can see you!

Her friends saw her home.

see   saw

buy

dance

see   about

Cut

Understand the word

I see

Write the word in a sentence

I can see for miles from up here

Color the word

Enter

Введіть

Find and circle the word

She saw him enter the room.

Please knock before entering

The project is entering its final stages

enter   saw
                          buy
          dance

entering   about
          entering

Understand the word

They entered into the classroom

Write the word in a sentence

You have to enter password to access the database

Color the word

Cry

Плакати

Find and circle the word

"don't cry," she said.

She skinned her knee and began to cry

She cried out in pain as she fell

cry   saw

cry

dance

cried   about

climbs

Understand the word

she is crying

Write the word in a sentence

She cried bitter tears when she got the letter.

Color the word

Climb

Піднімайтеся

Find and circle the word

To climb the stairs

They climbed into the truck and drove away

I've made three climbs so far this year.

climbed   saw

climb

dance

entering   about

climbs

Understand the word

Climb to the top of the hill

Write the word in a sentence

To climb the mountain

Color the word

Build

Будувати

Find and circle the word

Without a plan, you can't build a house

Some owls had built a nest in the chimney

We decided to build on high ground, above the river

built   saw
                    build
          dance
build   about
        climbs

Understand the word

Construction worker built a wall

Write the word in a sentence

He moved to London where he built up a successful career

Color the word

Complete Завершено

Find and circle the word

Her family completed the list of guests

I *need two more cards to complete the set*

Complete the sentence with one of the
adjectives provided

completed   saw

complete

dance

complete   about

climbs

Understand the word

Project completed

Write the word in a sentence

The baby completed our
family

Color the word

Laugh | Смійся

Find and circle the word

I couldn't stop laughing

They laughed at her jokes.

I laughed till I cried.

laughed   saw   laughed

dance

complete   climbs   laughing

Understand the word

I laughed

Write the word in a sentence

That guy always makes me

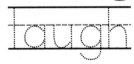

Color the word

Draw   # Намалювати

Find and circle the word

Sam *can draw very well*

Anna drew an elephant

Draw a line at the bottom of the page

draw   saw

draw

dance

complete   drew

climbs

Understand the word

I draw

Write the word in a sentence

The children drew pictures of their families.

Color the word

Talk

Поговорити

Find and circle the word

My little girl has just started to talk

The two sides have agreed to talk

Talk won't get us anywhere

talk   saw

                    talk

          dance

talk   drew

          climbs

Understand the word

I had a talk with my boss

Write the word in a sentence

I've heard talk of a layoff

Color the word

Read	Прочитайте

Find and circle the word

She read slowly and quietly It's not brilliant but it's worth a read I read the book over the weekend.	read saw read read talk drew climbs

Understand the word

I read...

Write the word in a sentence

She couldn't read or write

Color the word

Listen

Слухайте

Find and circle the word

What kind of music do you listen to?

You haven't listened to a word I've said!

Listen to this

Listen   saw

listened

read

listen   drew

climbs

Understand the word

I listen...

Write the word in a sentence

Have a listen to this! I've never heard anything like it before

Color the word

Play	Грати

Find and circle the word

He learned to play the clarinet

The ball had gone out of play

She played the ace of spades

play   saw   played   read   play   climbs   drew

Understand the word

I play football

Write the word in a sentence

Which team do you play for?

Color the word

Touch | Дотик

Find and circle the word

Don't touch the machine when it's in use

That paint is wet, so don't touch

She can't touch the fire

touch   saw
                touch
        read

play   touch
    climbs

Understand the word

I touch the leaf

Write the word in a sentence

Push the bookcases together until they touch

Color the word

Wait

Зачекайте

Find and circle the word

We need to wait in line for the tickets

Wait here for me – I'll be back in a minute

The dentist kept me waiting for ages

touch   saw

wait

waiting

play   climbs   wait

Understand the word

I'm waiting for the bus

Write the word in a sentence

An envelope was waiting for me when I got home.

Color the word

Open

ВІДЧИНЕНО

Find and circle the word

You left the container open

Someone had left the window wide open

The supermarket is open till 8.00 p.m

open   saw

open

waiting

play   climbs   open

Understand the word

I opened the window

Write the word in a sentence

Make sure you have both files open at the same time.

Color the word

Exit

ВИЙШОВ

Find and circle the word

The character exits stage right

Click here to save and exit

Remember to save your work before you exit

exits

saw

open

waiting

exit

exit

climbs

Understand the word

I exited the building

Write the word in a sentence

Remember to save your work before you exit

Color the word

Eat

Ïсти

Find and circle the word

What do you want to eat for lunch?

We usually eat at about 7 p.m.

Do you eat meat?

eat   saw

eat

waiting

exit   eat

climbs

Understand the word

I eat...

Write the word in a sentence

She eats pizza

Color the word

Hug | обійняти

Find and circle the word

He hugged me

Hug me more

Father hugging his daughter

think   with

Hug

hugged

hugging   for

cook

Understand the word

I hug my mom

Write the word in a sentence

**me tight**

Color the word

You

ТИ

Find and circle the word

You are a student

Next to you

We will go with you

you   yes   you   can   you   no   one

Understand the word

You are my best friend

Write the word in a sentence

Do you **want to play with us**

Color the word

Can	можна

Find and circle the word

I can do it	can eat
Can i sit	go
Can Sam come over?	can
	can about
	ask

Understand the word

You can do it

Write the word in a sentence

 **I go out**

Color the word	
Cook	готувати

Find and circle the word

Won't he cook?

I can cook

Alen is cooking

two   yes

cook

can

Cooking   for

cook

Understand the word

I cook

Write the word in a sentence

Sam cooks **his favorite dish**

Color the word

Think	думати

Find and circle the word

I think healthy food is important to health

I think the internet has a few downsides

I think there are some errors

think   with
                think
        can
think   for
        cook

Understand the word

I think it's a good idea

Write the word in a sentence

I  **it's a nice book**

Color the word

Find	Знайти

Find and circle the word

couldn't find Alan's phone number.

Vitamin C is found in citrus fruit.

I had a map but I still couldn't find my way back to the hotel.

find   saw

find

waiting

exit   found

climbs

Understand the word

I found a masterpiece

Write the word in a sentence

She doesn't find it easy to talk about her problems

Color the word

Carry

Hece

Find and circle the word

Would you like me to carry your bag for you?

These books are too heavy for me to carry

we were able to carry it onto the car

carry   saw

              carry

     waiting

exit   carry

      climbs

Understand the word

I carry...

Write the word in a sentence

Would you like to carry my bag?

Printed in Great Britain
by Amazon